Bug Watching

with Charles Henry Turner

by Michael Elsohn Ross

illustrations by
Laurie A. Caple

 Carolrhoda Books, Inc./Minneapolis

To Matteo, for all his questions—M. E. R.

For my son Ethan, whose curiosity is contagious—L. A. C.

The author wishes to thank Kevin Grace at the University of Cincinnati Archives; Minnie Clayton and Gwendolyn Walker at Clark Atlanta University; Sharon Huffman, Augustine Porter, and Donald Shipp of the St. Louis Public Schools; Dennis Northcott of the Missouri Historical Society; and finally, Jean Turner.

The illustrator wishes to thank Steven J. Krauth, Senior Academic Curator, Insect Research Collection, Department of Entomology, University of Wisconsin–Madison.

Carolrhoda Books, Inc., c/o The Lerner Publishing Group
241 First Avenue North, Minneapolis, MN 55401 U.S.A.

LIBRARY OF CONGRESS CATALOGING-IN-PUBLICATION DATA

Ross, Michael Elsohn
  Bug watching with Charles Henry Turner / by Michael Elsohn Ross ; illustrated by Laurie A. Caple.
    p. cm. —(Naturalist's apprentice)
  Includes index.
  ISBN 1-57505-003-X
  1. Insects—Experiments—Juvenile literature. 2. Arachnida—Experiments—Juvenile literature. 3. Turner, Charles Henry—Juvenile literature. I. Caple, Laurie A. II. Title. III. Series: Ross, Michael Elsohn, Naturalist's apprentice.
QL467.2.R66 1997
595.7—dc20   96-11972

Manufactured in the United States of America
1 2 3 4 5 6 - JR - 02 01 00 99 98 97

TIGER SWALLOWTAIL
BUTTERFLIES

Contents

Chapter 1
Bug Watching

RED-LEGGED LOCUST

Bugs are everywhere! They hop, crawl, and zoom through our houses and neighborhoods. They dine out in our gardens and make homes in our backyards. Though some bugs, such as buzzing houseflies, are difficult to ignore, many lead quiet and secretive lives. Perhaps you have already spied on some of them. Maybe you have followed cruising ants or springing grasshoppers. As you watched them, did you wonder what they were up to? Were you curious about their habits and home life? Imagine what it would be like to investigate bug questions such as these your whole life. Could you see yourself becoming a famous bug watcher?

Charles Henry Turner was an expert bug watcher who started wondering about bugs when he was a small boy. He was born on February 3, 1867, in Cincinnati, Ohio, less than two years after the Civil War ended. By the time Charles was in school, he was bugging his teachers with bug questions. As he watched a little creature, he couldn't help but wonder. What is it? Where is it going? How does it find its way? What does it eat? The questions just bubbled forth. Charles had begun to ask the questions of a **naturalist,** or a student of nature.

Years later, after Charles had become an important naturalist, he told a friend that one of his teachers had finally said to him when he was a boy, "If you want to know all about these things, why don't you go and find out?"

Young Charles had answered, "I will."

This is the story of how he found out.

What's a Bug?

Any small crawly creature can be called a bug. Bugs with six legs and three main body parts are insects. Bugs with eight legs and two main body parts are spiders or spider relatives. Scientists call insects such as stinkbugs "true bugs." These true bugs have needle-like sucking mouthparts and x-like crosses on their backs. If you lift the upper wing of a true bug, you can see that the top half is hard and leathery and the lower half is thin and clear. Can you find any true bugs around your home?

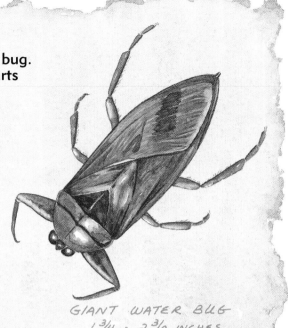

GIANT WATER BUG
1 3/4 - 2 3/8 INCHES

During and after the Civil War, great changes occurred all over America. The greatest change of all was that slaves were freed. Blacks who had been enslaved on Southern plantations or who had escaped to safety in Canada were free to go where they wanted. By law, they could get jobs, go to school, and even buy a home if they could afford one.

Many African Americans were on the move. Among them were Charles's parents, who moved to Cincinnati. Addie Campbell Turner came from neighboring Kentucky, which had been a slave state. Thomas Turner moved south from his birthplace in Toronto, Canada. Just over the border from the United States, Toronto had been a safe place for runaway slaves.

Cincinnati was a busy and prosperous river town. Boats steamed up and down the wide Ohio River carrying iron ore from the Great Lakes and tobacco and cotton from the South. This growing city had jobs for people who were willing to work hard even though the wages were low. Laborers were needed on the docks and steamboats. There was work for servants in restaurants and homes. Unfortunately, the earnings from these jobs were barely enough to pay for food and rent.

Many people came to Cincinnati in the 1860s hoping to find work.

African Americans had their freedom, but they did not have a lot of choices. Even if they were skilled in a craft, such as shoemaking or carpentry, they were often forced to accept other low-paying work because many white business owners refused to hire skilled black workers. Blacks did not have the right to vote. They were forced to attend all-black schools and to use separate hospitals and streetcars.

Most white women didn't have jobs outside the home at that time. But since black families' earnings were low, many African-American women had to work outside the home to earn extra money. Mrs. Turner was a nurse and worked for some of the leading families in town, while Mr. Turner worked as the custodian of a church. These two jobs gave the Turners money to spare. With their extra money, the Turners could afford to buy books. Charles's father had a love for learning and was known in his community as a thinker. In the 1870s, books were expensive, and few families—black or white—had home libraries. The Turners worked hard and filled their bookshelves with several hundred books. Little Charles wanted to read them all!

Even though Charles's family had a large collection of books, Charles did not have access to many books on bugs. Very few books about bugs had even been written. Without books, it was not only difficult to identify bugs, but it was hard to get basic information about what they ate and where they lived.

Choosing a Field Guide

Unlike Charles, you'll most likely find plenty of books about bugs. But you may need help figuring out how to select books that will be most useful. Here are some features of field books that will be helpful in telling little buglike creatures apart. After some practice, you'll be able to tell a dragonfly from a snakefly and a bark louse from a bark beetle.

✔ Illustrations vs. Photos
Believe it or not, a drawing or painting usually shows more detail than a photo. Go for a book with illustrations.

✔ The Whole Gang
Find a book that includes all the species, or kinds, of bugs that live in your region, not just the common ones. The more creatures your field guide lists, the more likely you'll be able to find information about the uncommon creatures that you might bump into in your own backyard or house.

✔ User-Friendly
Choose a guide that is easy to use. If the pictures and descriptions are all on one page, you'll be better able to make a quick identification.

✔ In the Pocket
An encyclopedia of insects might be jam-packed with information, but it's a heavy load to carry on bug expeditions. A guide that can slip into your back pocket or fit easily into a daypack is just right. Of course, a larger book is nice to use at home if you can capture live creatures and bring them back for a short visit.

✔ Get the Facts
The first few times you go bug watching, simply flip through your field guide until you find a picture that matches each bug you see. Keep the book in a handy place where you can flip through it regularly. Soon you'll know where in the book to turn, and you'll be able to make lightning-quick identifications.

BALD FACED
HORNET NEST

Chapter 2
Homemaking

By the time Charles entered school in the early 1870s, life was improving for African Americans. Black men, such as Charles's father, were allowed to vote and exercise other rights as citizens. This was a big change for men who had once been slaves without any rights. (Women across the country—black and white—were not given the right to vote until 1920.) But inequality between blacks and whites still existed. Blacks had to attend schools and churches separate from whites and were banned from many restaurants and hotels. It was a society that was far from equal. But as African Americans exercised their right to vote, some conditions, such as education, got better.

Charles attended one of the three elementary schools open to black children in Cincinnati. Fortunately for him, the city's black schools were the best available to African Americans in Ohio. Charles also had the opportunity to attend high school. At the time Charles was growing up, Cincinnati had only one black high school. The school was overcrowded, but the teachers were dedicated. Charles graduated from Gaines High School at the top of his class.

Most colleges and universities in the 1880s did not accept black students. The University of Cincinnati was a public institution, and though it had no laws forbidding the entrance of black students, few were admitted. Charles applied, and in 1886, he became a student at the University of Cincinnati. He was the only African American in his class. Charles's first year at the university was a challenge. He had a particularly hard time with his math, chemistry, and German classes, and his grades were low that first year.

Charles made time in his life for things other than school. In 1887, he married Leontine Troy, who was also from Cincinnati. Despite the new responsibilities of being a husband, Charles's grades improved. His enthusiasm for learning soon earned him the respect of his professors and fellow students. In the spring of 1888, he took a leave of absence from the university to teach fifth grade at a school in Indiana. It is not known why he left. Perhaps he needed money for school and to support his new wife.

Charles resumed his studies at the University of Cincinnati in the fall of 1889. Still interested in animals, he found his way to the biology department laboratory run by Dr. C. L. Herrick. Inside Professor Herrick's busy lab, students investigated and compared the

Very few African-American students attended the University of Cincinnati in the 1880s and 1890s.

brains, nerves, and behavior of various creatures. Charles studied hard. Even though he worked as a substitute teacher besides attending school, his grades steadily improved.

Have you ever been called a birdbrain? Charles Henry Turner might have thought this was a compliment. In Dr. Herrick's lab, Charles had the chance to study the brains of birds. Like other researchers, he discovered that bird brains are actually quite remarkable. The brains of birds are large in comparison to their bodies, which means that they are capable of more complex thoughts and behavior than other animals of equal size. Charles discovered so much from his bird-brain studies that he published a hundred-page article. Professor Herrick was impressed by Charles's abilities.

One day Dr. Herrick and his wife decided that they would like to serve tea and cakes to the laboratory students on Fridays. But Dr. Herrick worried that some students might feel uncomfortable sharing a table with Turner. Many of Herrick's students were from Southern families who believed blacks shouldn't socialize with whites. Would they object to having tea with Charles because of their prejudice toward blacks?

Dr. Herrick asked some of Charles's fellow students how they felt. To his surprise, he discovered that not only were they glad to have tea with Turner, they looked up to him as the most outstanding student at the lab. Charles was shy and quiet, but he was well liked. Every Friday from then on, a white tablecloth was set out on one of the lab tables, and the students shared their research reports. Even though Charles experienced prejudice and inequality outside of school, he found friends and new opportunities at the lab. In 1890, Herrick offered Charles a job as a lab assistant. He accepted and became the only African American on the faculty of the university.

Find Some Bug Partners

You too can join a community of bug scientists. You may have noticed other kids in your neighborhood or school exploring trails of ants or playing with grasshoppers. Next time you meet one of these bugologists, ask what's up and see if you can join in. Perhaps you can share books, tools, or most important, your ideas. If you have a computer at school or home with online capabilities, you can even link up with bug scientists in other parts of the country—or the world. For information on bug networks, contact the Young Entomologists' Society, 1915 Peggy Place, Lansing, MI 48910-2553, (517) 887-0499. (The Young Entomologists' Society has a small membership fee.)

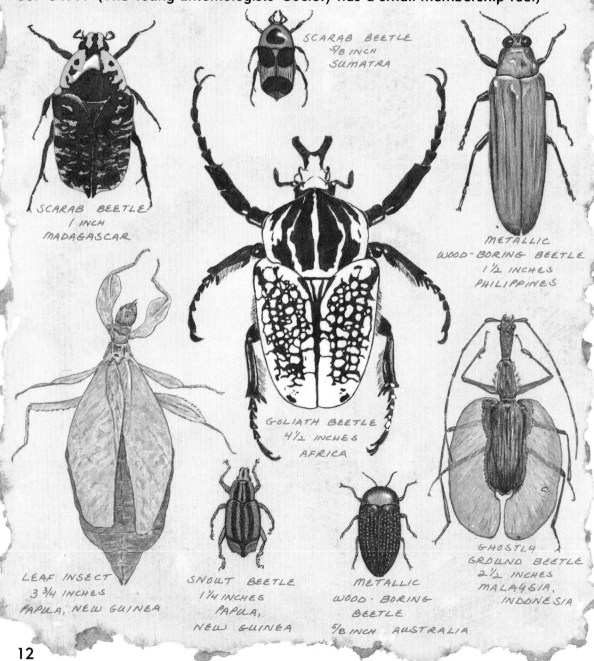

SCARAB BEETLE
⅝ INCH
SUMATRA

SCARAB BEETLE
1 INCH
MADAGASCAR

METALLIC
WOOD-BORING BEETLE
1½ INCHES
PHILIPPINES

GOLIATH BEETLE
4½ INCHES
AFRICA

LEAF INSECT
3¾ INCHES
PAPUA, NEW GUINEA

SNOUT BEETLE
1¼ INCHES
PAPUA,
NEW GUINEA

METALLIC
WOOD-BORING
BEETLE
⅝ INCH AUSTRALIA

GHOSTLY
GROUND BEETLE
2½ INCHES
MALAYSIA,
INDONESIA

Do you think of scientists as reclusive people who work all alone? It's only in movies that scientists hide out in laboratories tucked away in the towers of castles. Without lab partners and access to scientific journals and books, most scientists would find it very difficult to make amazing discoveries. Like other great scientists, Charles Henry Turner kept in touch with fellow workers and read about new discoveries in German, French, Italian, and English journals. He shared his own ideas with other researchers in the numerous articles he wrote.

The Well-Equipped Bug Watcher

Charles Henry Turner made use of a variety of equipment when he went bug exploring. A magnifying lens allowed him to look closely at bugs. Notebooks were handy for recording observations and questions. Empty jars (with holes in the lids) were great for housing live insects that he wanted to study at home. To be a well-equipped bug watcher, gather some of the items below. Happy bug watching!

magnifying lens

sun hat

daypack with notebook, water bottle, and snacks

plastic bug bottle

comfortable shoes

During his last year at the University of Cincinnati, Charles Henry Turner spied on gallery spiders. Perhaps you've noticed their flat sheets of silk scattered on lawns and fields, or attached to the outside walls of a house. Above each spiderweb are crisscrossing lines that look like an obstacle course for flies. If you look more closely, you'll notice a narrow funnel, or gallery, at the end of the sheet. The spider hangs out in this funnel. These spiders are no longer known as gallery spiders as they were in Turner's time, but are called funnel weavers because of their funnels.

Like other spiderwebs, funnel webs can be deadly traps. Grasshoppers, flies, and other bugs who mistakenly crash-land in these silken airfields soon find themselves caught by fine threads. As they struggle, the vibrations of the web alert the spider lurking in the funnel. In a flash, it races over the sheet and ties up the tangled victim. To see this amazing spider in action, just tickle a funnel web sheet with a grass stem and watch. If you do it gently enough, the spider will dash out in search of a meal.

Have you ever noticed a fly crashing into a window? Charles found one funnel web that looked like it was built just for catching window-crashing flies. Like a tightrope walker's net, it hung below the windowsill. Above it was a network of silk snare lines.

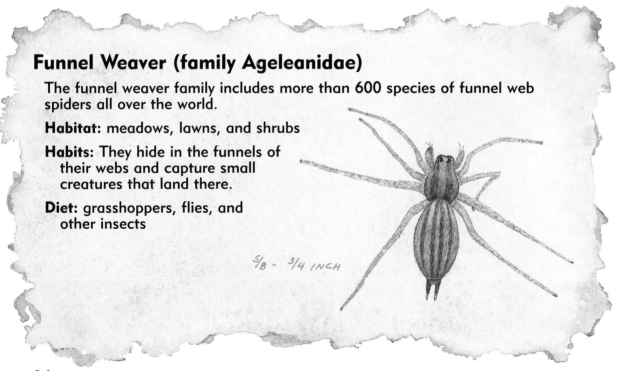

Funnel Weaver (family Ageleanidae)

The funnel weaver family includes more than 600 species of funnel web spiders all over the world.

Habitat: meadows, lawns, and shrubs

Habits: They hide in the funnels of their webs and capture small creatures that land there.

Diet: grasshoppers, flies, and other insects

5/8 - 3/4 INCH

When the flies bounced off the window, they collided with the snare lines and tumbled onto the sheet below. Charles was amazed. The spider had built a trap that was perfect for the spot! It appeared to Charles that each spiderweb he found was like a house built to fit its surroundings.

"Is this web the result of blind instinct? I think not," wrote Turner about one of the webs he studied. At that time, most scientists believed that spiders were little web-building machines. Like machines, they didn't think and they didn't have to learn. They just knew how to build webs, and they simply built them. This kind of automatic behavior is called **instinct.** A spider that builds only by instinct would build the same web each time, no matter what the building site looked like.

Charles wandered through fields looking at webs. The more he looked, the more he was convinced that each spider designed the best trap for its hunting grounds. It seemed to him that spiders were clever custom builders. Charles experimented to check his theory. In one test, he looked for spiders that had built webs of different shapes: triangular, rectangular, or irregular. Then he placed each of the spiders in a separate bottle. What do you think happened? All the webs the spiders made inside round bottles were round. But when placed in rectangular boxes, many of the same spiders made rectangular webs.

FUNNEL WEAVER SPIDERWEB

One day, Charles discovered a large triangular web in a corner, stretched between a windowsill and a wall. He decided to try another test. Charles took notes on the web's design, then swept the web away with a broom. He was careful not to hit the spider, though, because he meant it no harm. By the next morning, the spider had built a web almost exactly like the old one. Charles swept it away again. Two more times, the spider made webs of the same design, and each time Charles swept them away.

But the next time the spider spun a web, it made some major changes. Unlike the previous webs, this new narrow one was hidden under the overhanging windowsill. Charles wondered, "Was this variation mere chance, or did the spider realize there was danger beyond this sill and act accordingly?" Do you think the spider was trying to solve its web problem by changing the web's design?

Charles's investigation showed the creativity of funnel weavers. Each spider created a special trap for its own hunting grounds. Charles thought the spiders' actions showed **intelligence**—the spiders were responding to the challenges of each situation. Charles concluded that spiders are guided by instinct to build a web, but they seem to use intelligence when adding the fine touches.

Web Museum

Have you ever looked closely at a spiderweb? Each one is delicate but deadly (if you're a bug!). Each one is a work of art. Like a visitor to an art museum, take a tour to study the variety of web designs in your own habitat.

Supplies
✔ a notebook and pencil
✔ a tape measure or ruler

ORB WEAVER
SPIDER

What to Do
Search for webs around the inside and outside of your house. Observe each web as if it were a famous sculpture. Make a sketch of the basic shape and design of each web and measure its size (without disturbing the web). This will help you to notice differences between webs. When you find webs that seem to be made by the same kind of spider, compare the size and shape of the webs. Are they different? Do they seem to be designed for the building site? Take a family member or a friend along on your tour. Challenge them to appreciate the fine art of their eight-legged neighbors.

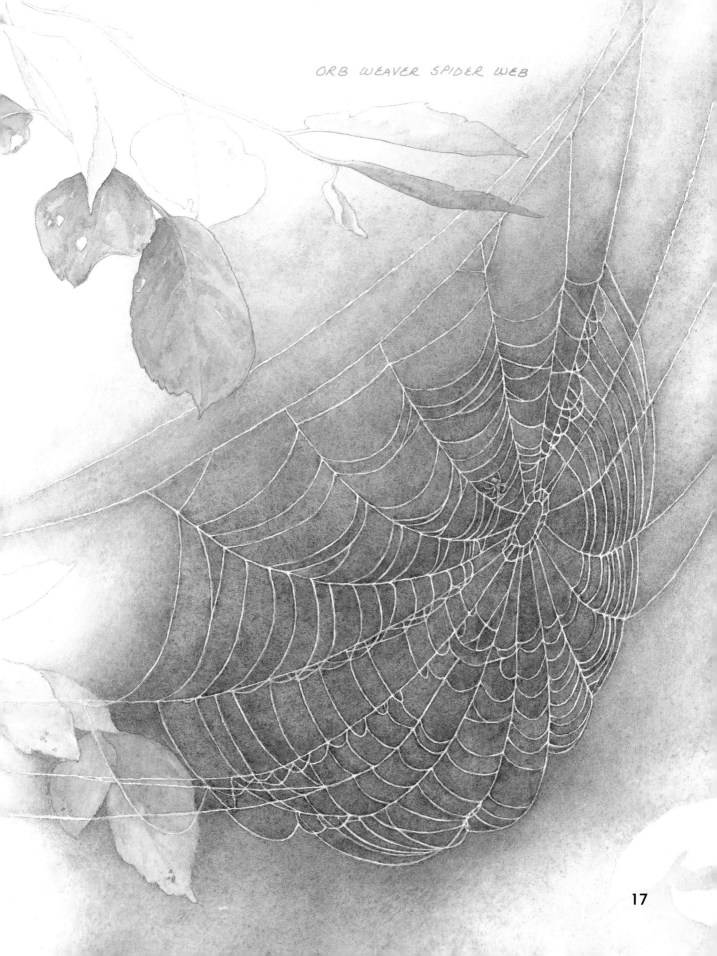

ORB WEAVER SPIDER WEB

INDIA LEAF BUTTERFLY
(ON BRANCH)

Chapter 3
Home Finding

In January of 1892, Leontine gave birth to a daughter, Louisa Mae. Charles graduated from the University of Cincinnati that June with a master of science degree in biology. The Turners then moved to Atlanta, Georgia, where Charles had a new job as professor of biology at Clark University.

Clark was a small college for black students. Like many other black colleges, Clark had started after the Civil War as an elementary school to educate freed slaves. By the 1880s, it also offered high school and college programs. Like other black schools, it was always short of money. Over two-thirds of the state education money in Georgia went to white colleges, even though almost half the people in Georgia were black. The teachers at Clark were poorly paid, and there was not enough money for even basic laboratory equipment or a science library.

At the University of Cincinnati, Charles had become used to working in a modern lab with other scientists. At Clark, Charles found that running a one-man science department with little money was a challenge. Few other African Americans had college degrees, and even fewer had degrees in science. In fact, not many black colleges even offered science classes. But Charles had high hopes for his students. Using his own money, Charles made homemade devices and tools for the lab. With this basic lab equipment, he introduced students to the principles of modern science. Despite the lack of books and materials, Charles was able to train his students to become scientists. One student even published his research report in a well-known science journal.

Even though Charles didn't have other scientists to work with at the school in Atlanta, he had the opportunity to meet other well-educated African Americans for the first time. John Wesley Bowen, the second African American to earn a doctorate (the highest university degree), and W. E. B. Du Bois, a famous scholar and civil rights leader, both taught at colleges in Atlanta. A debate about the education of African Americans arose among these educated African Americans. Du Bois argued that everyone, white or black, should have the same educational opportunities. Booker T. Washington, another well-known educator, didn't think this was possible at that time. He believed that full equality would take a long time and that African Americans needed to concentrate on learning practical skills rather than worrying about equality.

W. E. B. Du Bois

Booker T. Washington

A new organization called the National Association for the Advancement of Colored People (NAACP) was eventually formed, and Charles joined. The NAACP supported the African-American move for total equality. As a teacher, Charles Henry Turner encouraged his students to pursue their interests and to succeed in spite of racial prejudice.

As more African Americans became educated and owned their own businesses or farms, they came under attack by prejudiced whites. Some blacks had their property destroyed. Others were accused of crimes, and angry mobs sometimes killed them by hanging before they could have a fair trial. In Georgia, rich white landowners were short of farm labor. They convinced the state legislature to pass a law that allowed them to use prisoners as farm workers. Many African Americans were falsely convicted of crimes so these white farmers could have enough prisoners to work in their fields. Leaders such as W. E. B. Du Bois risked their own lives by speaking out against these injustices.

Life was also hard for the Turner family. In 1895, Charles's wife, Leontine, died. For seven months before she died, she suffered from severe mental illness. Charles was left with three children, Louisa Mae, Owen, and Darwin, to raise on his own. Somehow Charles managed to teach school and care for his children at the same time.

Despite the hardships, home life for the Turner children was always an adventure. Bees, ants, cockroaches, and snakes were household guests. Books about animals filled the bookshelves. Charles took his children on nature walks. He introduced them to the language of pigeons and the ways of wasps.

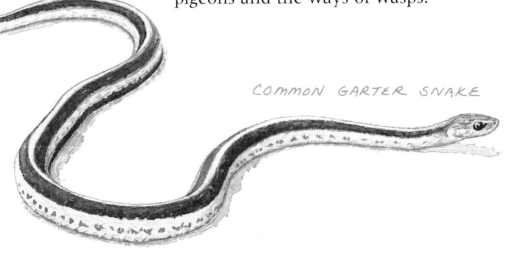

COMMON GARTER SNAKE

How to Operate a Magnifying Lens

You can get a bug's-eye view of the world with a magnifying lens, but that view may be a bit fuzzy unless you know how to operate your lens. Follow these steps and you'll soon be eye-to-eye with some of the strangest sights on Planet Earth.

✔ Hold the lens up in front of one eye and close the other. If you can't keep your eye closed, use your finger to hold the lid shut.

✔ Stand with your face toward the light (from a lamp or the sun) and look through the lens at anything up close. Lenses work best when they are held close to your eye, so always move toward what you are viewing with the lens held in front of your eye.

GOLDSMITH BEETLES

    Charles shared his curiosity about bugs and his excitement for research with his children. A scientist who studies insects is called an **entomologist.** It must have been fun for the Turner children to have an entomologist dad!

    In 1898, Charles went back to school again. He entered the University of Chicago to continue his studies. He began working toward a doctorate in **zoology,** the study of animals. It usually takes several years to earn a doctorate, and Charles couldn't do it all at once. He stayed in Chicago for one year, but then returned to his teaching job at Clark University full of energy.

One day, Charles noticed a trail of ants going up and down a brick post on the front porch of his Georgia home. When he followed the ants, he discovered that they were collecting honeydew from small insects called aphids on a nearby vine. Honeydew is a sweet liquid that aphids produce as they drink plant sap. Ants love to eat it. An ant would carry the honeydew in its **crop,** a pouch near its stomach, to a nest opening in the porch. At the nest, the ant would regurgitate, or throw up, the honeydew to share it with the other ants.

When Charles noticed a single ant on a leaf, he decided to use it in an experiment. Gently, he tore off the leaf and gave the ant a ride to a spot two feet away from the nest hole. He then poked the leaf stem into a crevice between the bricks and settled down to watch the ant. Would it go directly to the nest hole or not?

At first the ant acted as if it were dead. Then it walked about the leaf. Finally, the ant crawled off the leaf onto the pillar and went down, down, down away from the nest, almost all the way to the ground. It turned right. It turned left. Then it zigzagged all the way back up to the leaf. Up it went onto the leaf, and there it paraded around again before wandering onto the pillar once more. It went up and down the pillar again and once more returned to the leaf.

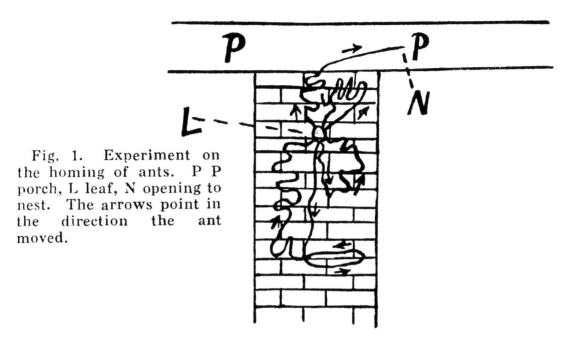

Fig. 1. Experiment on the homing of ants. P P porch, L leaf, N opening to nest. The arrows point in the direction the ant moved.

This illustration appeared with Turner's article on the homing of ants.

After a few more visits to the leaf and more wanderings on the pillar, the ant finally ambled up toward the nest. When it was close to its nest, it seemed to finally know the way. Like a horse nearing a barn, it sped up and cruised right in the entrance. The whole search for a nest two feet away had taken thirty minutes.

Many people believed that there was a mysterious power, the homing instinct, that guided certain animals on their travels. Ants were thought to be one of these animals. An animal with a homing instinct would have known exactly where its home was and gone straight to it. But look at Turner's map of the roving ant. It looks more like a pile of cooked spaghetti than a straight line. After Turner tried several other experiments on the homing instinct, he could find no evidence that ants had it. If ants don't use the homing instinct, how do they get home? Charles wanted to find out.

One well-known German scientist believed that ants left a special odor trail as they traveled about. When they wanted to go back home, they would simply follow the smell of their trail home like robots. Charles questioned this idea of bugs as little machines. He wondered if they were really led to and fro by smell.

To test this scent theory, Turner put ants on stage. This was not the kind of stage actors perform on, but a small ant-sized stage made of cardboard that would help him study the ants' movements. To allow the ants to go up or down from the stage, he designed cardboard ramps that he could rearrange. Charles knew that if he removed ants and their young from their nest and placed them on the stage, the ants would immediately begin to search for home. When young ants are taken from home, adult ants quickly haul them back to the safety of the nest.

Turner first provided only one ramp for the ants to walk down. After some wandering, they located the nest and began making trips back and forth to rescue their offspring. Were they following odor trails? If they were, do you think there would be an odor trail on the ramp?

Next Charles turned the ramp around so that the end that had been nearest to the nest was attached to the platform. If there was a scent trail on the ramp, he figured that the ants would become confused. What do you think happened? Nothing! The ants went down the ramp as if nothing were different. Charles repeated this test twelve times with five different kinds of ants, and the result was the same each time.

In another series of experiments, Charles placed new groups of ants and their young on a stage. Once they had walked down the path to the nest several times, he added a second ramp to the other side of the stage. The ants continued to use the old ramp and ignored the new one. After a while, Charles switched the ramps.

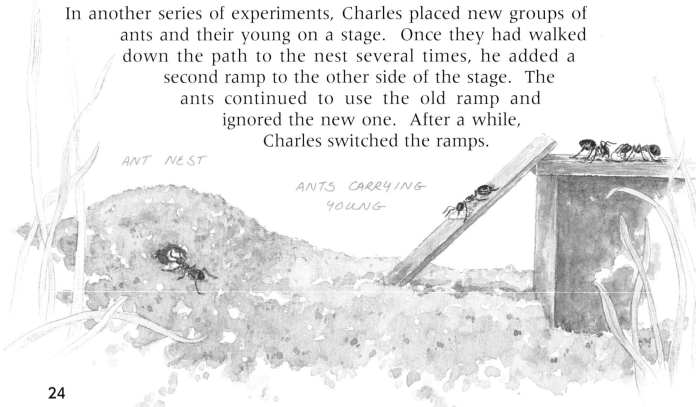

ANT NEST

ANTS CARRYING YOUNG

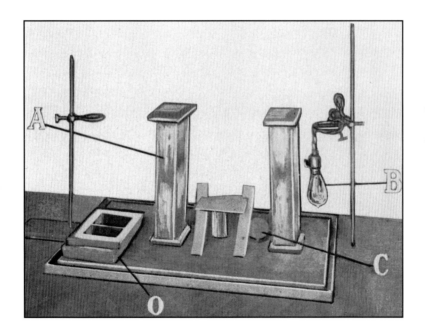

This illustration shows the setup for Charles's experiment to test ants' reaction to light. Note the stage in the center. A is a heat filter. B is a light. C is a mirror to show the underside of the ramp.

This time the new ramp was where the old one had been. Would the ants act confused when they encountered the ramp that had never been walked on? Would they wander about until they either found the old ramp or learned a way to get down the new one? What do you think happened?

Once again, the ants acted as if absolutely nothing had changed. They marched down the new ramp just like they had down the old one. Charles made one hundred similar tests using five different kinds of ants and got the same results each time. He now knew that ants use more than scent to find their way. The fact that they didn't even pause when the ramps were switched proved that something other than scent was giving them directions to the nest.

Charles wondered if the ants' sense of direction was affected by light. He placed a lamp on either side of the stage. To block the heat from the bulbs, he set filters between the stage and the lamps. He wanted to test the ants' reaction to light—not heat. When he first placed the ants and young on the stage, he had only one lamp turned on. After the ants had made many trips back and forth to the nest, he turned off the first lamp and turned on the lamp on the opposite side. What do you think happened? "In each case," wrote Turner, "the halting movements of the ants showed that they were disturbed."

Ant (family Formicidae)

There are more than 9,500 different species of ants worldwide!

Habitat: all types of places from deserts to tropical rain forests. They are common in backyards and houses.

Habits: All ants live in **colonies,** or large settlements. Some colonies contain more than 3,000,000 ants. Ant society is divided into **castes,** or groups, containing workers (females), queens (the ants that lay eggs for the colony), and males.

Diet: Ants are scavengers, which means they eat just about any food they find. They eat fungi, sap, seeds, leaves, and dead or live animals. Different species prefer certain foods over others. Some like sweets, while others choose seeds or meat.

Metamorphosis: Have you ever uncovered an ant nest when you moved a log or rock? Did you notice that the ants quickly snatched up little white bundles and hauled them to safety? These bundles are the ants' young. Ants go through several stages of development to become adult ants. This series of changes is called **metamorphosis.** Young ants hatch from tiny eggs into small, white wormlike **larvae.** After a couple of weeks, the larvae become **pupae.** During this stage, the ant slowly changes into an adult. The legless larvae and pupae both look like eggs, but the real eggs are actually too small to see well without magnification. Neither larvae nor pupae can walk, so the adult ants carry them if they need to be moved.

During the next five years, Charles did hundreds of experiments on ants. He changed the color of the ramps and discovered that some species of ants were disturbed by this while others were not. He changed the texture of ramps and found that some species were disturbed when a new ramp was smoother or rougher than a previous one. To test ants' reaction to odors, Charles placed strips of paper that had been soaked in a smelly substance, such as oil of cloves or oil of cedar, in the ants' path. The strips stopped the ants like an invisible wall. After a while, the ants would cross the cedar oil strips, but not the ones with oil of cloves. When he replaced the oil of cedar ramp with a plain one, the ants acted confused again.

Charles concluded from all these results that "ants are not slavishly guided by the scent of their footprints." He found that they are guided by smell, light, and touch, among other things. Do you think you could test Turner's conclusions?

Backyard Roadblocks

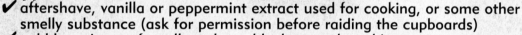

Supplies
✔ aftershave, vanilla or peppermint extract used for cooking, or some other smelly substance (ask for permission before raiding the cupboards)
✔ pebbles, pieces of cardboard, toy blocks, or other objects
✔ a notebook and a pen or pencil

What to Do
✔ Find a trail of ants in your backyard, local park, or schoolyard. Watch ants for a while and jot down some notes and questions about their actions. Where are they going? What are they doing?

✔ Choose something to use as a roadblock. This can be a strip of cardboard soaked with a scent, such as peppermint, or simply an object that makes a little wall, such as a toy block.

✔ Lay the roadblock flat on the ground across the ant trail. Do it carefully so that no harm comes to the ants. What happens? Why? Record your observations and questions in your notebook. Repeat the experiment at another ant trail. Do these ants react in the same way?

Warning
Some ants will bite or sting. Before experimenting with ants, ask a knowledgeable adult to help you select safe ants for your tests.

WHITE ADMIRAL BUTTERFLY

Chapter 4
Sensible Studies

DELAWARE SKIPPER BUTTERFLIES

In 1905, Charles took a job as principal of College Hill School in Cleveland, Tennessee. But after only one year in Tennessee, Charles returned to Chicago once more to finish his graduate studies. While he studied at the University of Chicago, Louisa Mae, Owen, and Darwin attended school back in Cincinnati, Ohio, and probably lived with relatives.

Charles's college education had started twenty years before. He had struggled through his math, chemistry, physics, and German classes. He had worked and started a family while he was studying. Most of his research had been done on his own, using equipment purchased from his own small salary. Finally in 1907, the University of Chicago awarded Charles Henry Turner a doctorate *magna cum laude* (with high praise) in zoology for his ant studies. This was a grand achievement. Charles was one of only a few African Americans who had earned this highest of all university degrees, and he had done it with special honors. Moreover, he had completed most of his studies at home, since he couldn't afford to attend the university full time, as most other students could.

In later years, W. E. B. Du Bois reported that after Charles had earned his doctorate, he was offered a teaching job at the University of Chicago by the head of the zoology department. Unfortunately, this man died shortly afterward. The new head professor refused to hire Turner because he "would not have a 'Nigger'" on the staff. So, despite Charles's excellent work at the university, he took a job teaching in a small school without an adequate laboratory.

Charles began work at Haines Normal School in Augusta, Georgia, teaching biology and chemistry to future teachers in 1907. He stayed in Augusta only a year, but it was long enough to meet and marry his second wife, Lillian Porter. His children had someone to help take care of them once more.

That same year, Charles was invited to the International Zoological Conference in Boston, where he read his report on the homing behavior of ants. He also served as secretary for the group of zoologists studying animal behavior. This was the only international conference that Turner attended. Most science professors who worked for universities were given money to travel to conferences, where they could meet and share information with other scientists from around the world. Charles had to pay his own way to such conferences out of his rather small salary.

In 1908, the Turners moved to St. Louis, Missouri, where they would live for the next fifteen years. Charles had a job teaching biology at Sumner High School and Teachers' College. Sumner was the only black high school in St. Louis. On Charles's first day at Sumner, some students came into his room, curious to see the new teacher. "What's your name, sir?" one asked. Turner erased some of the writing from the chalkboard and wrote his name. The students read aloud, "Dr. Charles Henry Turner, inorganic, not living matter." All of the kids laughed. The last phrase—*inorganic, not living matter*—was part of the writing that had not been erased.

STRIPE-TAILED VEJOVIS SCORPION

Charles was far from "inorganic, not living matter." He was lively, and he brought science alive for his students. His classroom, like his house, became a home for small creatures and plants that were collected for hands-on studies. Students were able to look through microscopes and use other lab equipment. Turner often used both hands at once to sketch pictures on the board in colored chalk. Other teachers often disciplined their students harshly, but Charles was gentle with his students. He treated them with respect and got it back. He was always available to students who needed extra help in any subject. On top of this, he took his students on field trips into the woods and fields near school. It's no wonder that his classroom may have gotten a little messy at times—and that he was pestered by his principal to keep it neater.

Schools in St. Louis, as in much of the South, were segregated. Black students and white students attended separate schools. Black students were usually taught by black teachers. Even though black schools got fewer supplies and their teachers earned less than teachers at white schools, schools like Sumner were the pride of the African-American community.

Charles Henry Turner's students knew he was a real scientist as well as a science teacher. Every summer he completed new experiments and shared the techniques and results with his classes. He wrote reviews of books for science magazines and published reports on his own experiments in journals such as *Biological Bulletin*. Other scientists around the country were impressed by Turner's work—and so were the local scientists who lived in St. Louis.

The St. Louis Academy of Science had always been an all-white organization. But this ended in 1910, when Charles Henry Turner was invited to join. This invitation was a supreme compliment to Turner's work and a bold social move on the part of the academy. At this time, most white citizens in St. Louis were pushing for more segregation of blacks and whites. Unlike the majority of other white citizens in St. Louis, members of the St. Louis Academy of Science failed to give in to these growing racist attitudes.

Since the 1890s, the rights of African Americans had been under attack. Laws were passed in Missouri prohibiting all marriages between blacks and whites. Black political leaders were barred from both Progressive and Republican Party meetings held in white-only hotels. Laws forcing the segregation of neighborhoods were passed. As Charles Henry Turner tried to understand the behavior of insects, he also wondered about the actions of humans.

During his summer vacation in 1910, Charles decided to tackle a seemingly simple question: were bees color-blind? For years, scientists who studied bees and flowers had assumed that bees could see color. But reports from scientists studying the structure of insect eyes suggested that bees and other insects had poor sight. "Can they really see colors or details?" asked these scientists. One German scientist wondered if bees found flowers solely by smell.

Charles Henry Turner began his investigations with some bees that were collecting nectar in a clover field near his home. Nectar is a sweet substance that flowers produce. Bees eat nectar and use it to make honey. Charles decided to use some fake flowers made from cardboard to test the color vision of bees. His first "flowers" were red cardboard circles attached to the tops of wooden rods. He placed six of these circles next to some clover flowers and then dribbled some honey on each one. Now the circles offered a sweet treat that bees like, just as the clover flowers did. Would bees collect honey from these fake flowers?

Honeybee (*Apis Mellifera*)

Honeybees are part of the family Apidae, the same family that bumblebees and digger bees belong to.

Habitat: lawns, meadows, orchards and gardens all over the world

Habits: Honeybees live in colonies with a queen bee, or the mother of the colony. They are one of the few insects that can be domesticated, or tamed by people.

Diet: Adult bees sip nectar from flowers. Larvae are fed honey and pollen by worker bees.

Warning: As you probably know, honeybees sting. Take care when you're around them. If you are allergic to bee stings, it's best to stay away.

3/8 - 5/8 INCHES

Charles sat nearby and watched. The first ten minutes went by, then twenty, and nothing happened. After thirty minutes, the bees continued to ignore the new flowers. But after two hours, a bee began to visit one of the circles. Soon another bee joined it, and then another. All three bees lapped up honey and then circled over the fake flower before flying back to the hive. There they would regurgitate the honey so other bees could store it.

The bees returned to the fake flower for more honey, and soon they began to visit two other circles. By this time Charles had to go home, so he collected all the fake flowers except the three that the bees were still feeding from. He recoated these with honey and left them for the bees. The next day, not only was all the honey gone, but it appeared as though some of the paper had been scraped off!

For his next experiment, Charles set out six red and six blue circles in the same places he had set them before. Some circles were attached to rods and some to weeds. He dabbed some honey in the center of each red circle, but he left the blue ones unsweetened. In an instant, a bee landed on one of the red "flowers." Within half an hour, the bees had made thirty-nine visits to the red circles and no visits to the blue ones. The bees continued to visit the red circles even when they were moved to new places. Why do you think the bees stayed away from the blue circles? Do you think they would visit blue circles sweetened with honey?

HONEYBEES

Charles dabbed a blue circle with honey to find out, and placed it near a red circle dabbed with honey. Although the bees kept visiting the red circle, they basically ignored the blue one for ten minutes before they finally began to feed from it. If bees found sweets just by smell, wouldn't the blue flower have been visited right away? Had the bees avoided the blue circle at first because they were used to finding honey on red flowers? Could bees really see color? These were questions that Charles asked.

To find answers, Charles continued experimenting with fake flowers. He made colored cardboard cones. He also made small boxes that had an open window and a tiny balcony for the bees to land on. Charles placed honey inside the cones and boxes where the bees couldn't see it. After many tests using these fake flowers, Charles discovered that once bees found honey on a fake flower, they would visit any other fake flower of the same color. It didn't matter if it had honey on it or not. On the other hand, the bees would pass by a new-colored flower at first, even if it was full of honey. Charles was becoming convinced that bees could see colors.

Can you tell when cookies are baking in the kitchen even when you are in another part of the house? Of course you can. Your nose tells your brain, "There are cookies in the oven." Charles discovered that it's the same with flower-visiting bees. When bees landed on balconies with boxes full of honey, they went right in the door. But when bees landed on empty boxes, they left without even looking inside for honey.

Charles concluded from his many tests that bees use more than one sense to get on target. They use color vision when they are far away and smell when they get closer. As usual, Charles showed that there are no simple answers. Bees don't find flowers by just sight or smell. They use both senses. Once again, Charles cleared up some mysteries that had confused his fellow scientists.

In another bee experiment, Charles Henry Turner wanted to find out if bees could tell what time of day it was. He set jam in dishes on an outdoor table three times a day (from 7:00 to 9:00 A.M., 12:00 to 2:00 P.M., and 5:00 to 7:00 P.M.). Bees came to the table for all three meals. But when Charles set out jam at breakfast time only, the bees still came for lunch and dinner, even though no jam was provided. After a while, they came only at breakfast time. From this simple test, Charles concluded that bees have a sense of time. This was later proved to be true by the experiments of other scientists. They showed that bees actually do visit flowers at certain times of the day, because flowers make nectar only at certain times. The bees visit the flowers when there is nectar, then go somewhere else when the flower stops making it for the day. Each day, the flowers make nectar at the same time, and the bees learn the schedule.

Flower Schedules

Supplies
✔ a notebook and pen or pencil
✔ a watch

What to Do
Find out if the bees in your community can tell time. Watch the flower-visiting bees in your neighborhood or in a park. Write down the time of day they visit each kind of flower. Do this for several days and then check your notes. Are there certain times when bees visit different types of flowers?

GOLDEN NORTHERN BUMBLEBEE

Louisa Mae Turner

Darwin R. Turner

Owen Turner

Chapter 5
Bug Clubhouse

During the early 1900s, many kids in St. Louis had a doghouse or henhouse at home. But the Turner kids were the only ones in the neighborhood whose dad had built an insectary. An entomologist's dream house, this small building had plenty of room for raising and housing insects. All the walls were windowless except for the screened north end. Inside the insectary there were tables, laboratory equipment, and, of course, lots of bugs.

What would your friends think if they came to your house and found out that your dad spent his time in a shack watching ant lions in jelly jars or running cockroaches through mazes? Louisa Mae, Turner's oldest child, was far from flustered by her dad's activities. She once said, "My father to us was just a plain, kind man who instilled in us those qualities that would make for the simple, successful life."

One type of insect that Charles Henry Turner kept in his insectary was the ant lion. Have you ever noticed funnel-shaped pits in the sand or in loose, dry soil? These pits are made by ant lion larvae. Even though they are small, ant lion pits are large enough that ants and other tiny creatures can tumble into them. Once inside, they try to clamber out, but many an unfortunate creature gets snatched by the ant lion larva waiting in ambush at the bottom. The ant lion sucks the body fluids of its **prey** through hollow jaws, before discarding its empty shell.

Charles began a three-year study of ant lions in 1912. During this time, he kept over five hundred of them, each in its own jar of soil. Only four articles on ant lions had appeared in American science journals when Charles began studying them. As in many of his other studies, Charles compared his observations with those of other scientists. For example, European writers had stated that ant lions shovel sand onto their heads with one of their front feet and then toss the sand out of the pit. Charles Henry Turner wrote, "In our American ant-lion, this pair of forelegs functions, not as a scrape, but as a brace to the body when the ant-lion is shovelling dirt or turning. Patient watching with a magnifying glass has failed to detect the fore-foot loading dirt upon the head. . . . The dirt gets upon the head by falling from above and from the sides, as the larva burrows backward through the soil. . . . The force with which an ant-lion tosses materials from its pit is astonishing. Often they are cast [thrown] several inches beyond the rim."

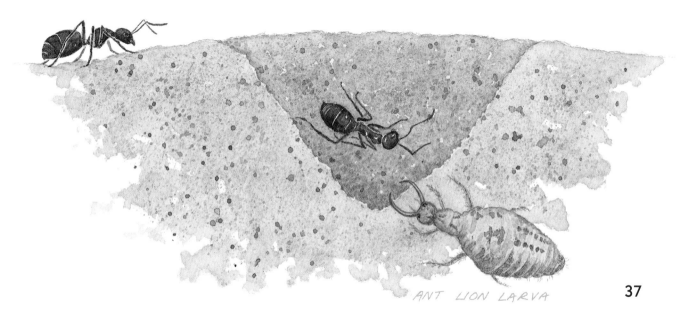

ANT LION LARVA

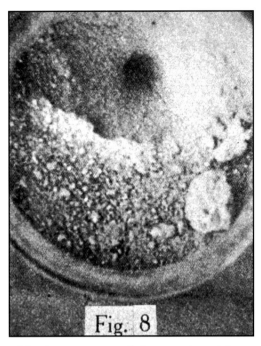

This photo accompanied Turner's article on ant lions.

Charles made many discoveries that showed that American ant lions were different from their European relatives. For instance, an American ant lion uses its rear end instead of its head to remove large dirt particles. With a load balanced on the rear of its abdomen, the ant lion would back up the side of its pit and dump the debris beyond the edges. Charles placed small pebbles in the pits and watched ant lions remove them. Instead of pushing forward like a bulldozer, they always backed the tiny boulders up and out. Charles eventually concluded that ant lion larvae can walk in only one direction—backwards!

Ant Lion (family Myrmeleontidae)

Ant lion larvae are commonly called doodlebugs. Ant lions are closely related to lacewings, snakeflies, and dobsonflies. Adult ant lions are similar in appearance to damselflies, except that they have softer bodies and long, clublike **antennae,** the sensing organs on their heads. The larvae are wingless and have large curved jaws.

Habitat: sand or dusty soil throughout most of North America and Europe

Habits: Ant lion larvae dig pits. The adults are attracted to lights at night.

Diet: Ant lion larvae munch any small creatures that blunder into their pits. Adults don't feed at all and live only long enough to mate.

LARVA
7/10 INCH

ADULT
1 3/4 INCHES

Through careful observation and simple experiments, Charles discovered more about the lives of ant lions. He found out that ant lion larvae develop faster when they eat more and that they lie still when shocked. Unlike other scientists, Charles concluded that ant lion larvae cause insects to fall to the bottom of the trap not by tossing soil at them, but by causing mini-landslides. Charles's twenty-five-page article on ant lions established him as an expert on these fascinating creatures.

Become a Bug Expert

How would you like to study a bug in the comfort of your own home? All you need is a bug, permission to bring it into the house, and a few materials. If you live in a cold climate, you may have trouble finding bugs in the winter. But you can often buy bugs from pet stores—they usually sell them as food for other creatures!

Supplies
✔ a clear plastic container or jar with tiny holes in the lid
✔ a magnifying lens
✔ a notebook and pen or pencil
✔ bug food, such as leaves or grass (if you notice your bug munching on anything when you catch it, provide it with some of the same food)

What to Do
Watch your bug in its container. How does it spend its day? Can you see it eating? Does it clean itself or take rests? Like a detective, keep track of the bug's movements and write down anything you notice about its behavior. Share your discoveries with your family and friends. After a couple of days, release your bug so it can continue its life in the wild. Don't release pet store bugs into the wild. If you don't want to keep them, return them to the store.

NORTHERN WALKING STICK

"Can a cockroach learn by trial and error?" Charles wondered. Learning by trial and error is the same as learning by successes and mistakes. For example, you may have learned how to control your parents' behavior by trying a variety of techniques until you learned what worked.

In the summer of 1912, Charles decided to test the learning abilities of cockroaches by running them through mazes. Inside his insectary, he set up a flat metal maze with four blind alleys. These alleys were like dead-end streets. The exit ramp attached to point C on the maze led to the jelly jar that the cockroach had been kept in. Once near its jar, the cockroach would immediately run inside, like a mouse escaping into its mouse hole.

The maze was propped up with glass rods above a pan of water. The only way down was by the ramp to the jelly jar. If the cockroaches jumped or tried to climb down the rods, they would end up getting a bath.

Each cockroach was placed on the maze by quickly flipping its jar upside down onto the starting point. When the cockroach had calmed down, Charles would slowly lift the jar and then take notes on the cockroach's movements. Any wrong turns or falls into the water were noted as mistakes. Each cockroach got a thirty-minute rest between tests, so it would not get too tired out. To remove any scent trail that a cockroach might have left, Charles wiped the maze clean with rubbing alcohol after each run.

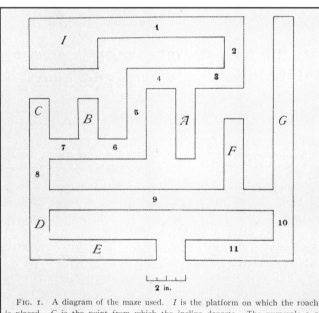

FIG. 1. A diagram of the maze used. *I* is the platform on which the roach is placed. *C* is the point from which the incline departs. The numerals 1–7 indicate the direct passageway to *C*. *A* is blind alley I., *B* is blind alley II., 8 *DE* is blind alley III. and 9 *FG* 10 11 is blind alley IV. of the tables.

Turner's cockroach maze

Cockroach (family Blattidae)

Cockroaches are closely related to crickets, praying mantises, walking sticks, and grasshoppers. There are over 3,500 species of cockroaches in the world.

Habitat: About 20 species of cockroaches live in human households and restaurants around the world and are considered pests.

Habits: Most common cockroaches like to hide in cracks and crevices during the day and come out at night. Cockroaches give off a strong odor.

Diet: garbage and plant debris

ORIENTAL
COCKROACH
1-1 ³/₈ INCHES

In an article about the experiment, Charles reported, "Upon being placed on the maze for the first time, a roach almost invariably rushes off into the water. Upon being replaced on the maze, it usually repeats the performance; some, however, do not rush into the water a second time. Sooner or later it stops rushing into the water and begins to search around for some other means of escape. It moves to and fro among the runways . . . enters blind alleys . . . makes its toilet one or more times, perhaps engages in a few acrobatic stunts, and finally, by accident, discovers the incline [slope] and passes down it to the glass cell that is its home."

The first few maze runs usually took fifteen to sixty minutes. On each run afterward, a cockroach would make fewer and fewer mistakes. Finally, after numerous trips and a few mistakes here and there, a cockroach could run the maze perfectly in one to four minutes. When a cockroach ran the maze three times in a row without mistakes, Charles decided that it had learned to solve the maze. Most cockroaches could learn the maze in a day but would forget it if kept away for more than twelve hours. The younger cockroaches ran the maze quicker than the older ones, but made more mistakes.

Charles noticed that maze-running cockroaches carefully examined corners and edges. Were they studying the route? After watching ten roaches perform, Charles concluded that the way they studied and gradually mastered the maze was proof that they indeed learned by trial and error. Charles once again showed that insects are not little robots. They learn in many of the same ways people do.

Maze Making

Do you have questions about the learning abilities of little creatures? You too can make a maze and investigate your questions!

Supplies
✔ blocks
✔ cardboard
✔ sheets of clear plastic
✔ modeling clay
✔ several clear plastic containers or jars (with small holes in the lids)
✔ bugs (see below for details)

What to Do
✔ To test the learning abilities of bugs, make a maze with blocks, cardboard, or other materials. Use modeling clay to hold your maze together and to fill in gaps the bugs could escape through. With a roof made of clear plastic, you can watch the bugs without them getting away.

✔ Decide what kind of bug you would like to test. Slow critters, such as caterpillars, may be easier to work with than speedy creatures like cockroaches. Do you think it will help to offer a prize, such as a favorite food, at the end of the maze? Perhaps caterpillars will go toward their favorite leaves. After you've tried slower creatures, you might want to try fast-moving ones, such as pill bugs. These might be even more exciting.

✔ Put a bug at the beginning of your maze and watch what it does. Whether you use slow or fast bugs, it is probably easiest to test them one at a time. Use your notebook to record the amount of time it takes each bug to run the maze. Then test the same bug again to see if it can run the maze faster. Keep your bugs in labeled containers, so you can keep track of which ones you have already watched.

WHITE-LINED SPHINX HORNWORM

MICROSCOPIC WATER FLEA

Charles Henry Turner had been as busy as a bee. Despite the long hours spent caring for his children, teaching, and running experiments, he had published forty-three scientific reports by the time he was fifty years old. Even though Charles Henry Turner was not teaching at the university level, his work was highly regarded by scientists in both Europe and the United States. All this discovery came to a brief halt when Charles became ill at age fifty-one. For several years, he struggled with poor health until he was finally well enough to experiment once again.

Charles was becoming more and more interested in the connections between bugs and their environments. This type of science, called **ecology,** was still a new science in the 1920s. To learn more about these relationships, Charles did some ecological investigations of water fleas and wasps. While his earlier research had established him as a pioneer in the study of animal behavior, these new studies marked him as one of the United States' early ecologists.

Unfortunately, Charles did not have a chance to get as far as he might have in his study of ecology. In 1923, at the age of fifty-six, Charles died as a result of his prolonged illness.

Although Charles Henry Turner was honored in St. Louis by having two schools named after him (Turner Middle School and Turner Open Air School), his amazing life and studies remain unknown to most Americans. But the boy who said "I will" made some amazing discoveries that we can still learn from. Despite the prejudice of his times, Charles Henry Turner followed his own paths to discovery, and in doing so, revealed a rich and intelligent world. Perhaps you too will get carried away by your fascination with bugs and wander like a curious ant through life's mysteries.

Charles Henry Turner (above) *had two schools in St. Louis named after him, including Turner Open Air School* (left), *which was later renamed Turner Middle Branch.*

Important Dates

1867—Charles Henry Turner was born in Cincinnati, Ohio, on February 3.

1886—Enters the University of Cincinnati

1887—Marries Leontine Troy

1890-92—Works as biology assistant at the University of Cincinnati

1891—Receives a bachelor of science degree from the University of Cincinnati

1892—Receives a master of science degree from the University of Cincinnati

1892—Louisa Mae Turner born

1893-1895—Darwin and Owen Turner born (birth dates unknown)

1893-1905—In charge of science department, Clark University, Atlanta, Georgia

1895—Wife, Leontine Troy Turner, dies

1905-1906—Serves as principal of College Hill School, Cleveland, Tennessee

1906-1907—Finishes Ph.D. at University of Chicago, *magna cum laude*

1907-1908—Teaches biology and chemistry at Haines Normal School in Augusta, Georgia. Marries Lillian Porter

1908—Begins a career as a science teacher at Sumner High School St. Louis, Missouri

1910—Elected a member of St. Louis Academy of Science—the first African-American member

1923—Dies on February 14

Glossary

antennae: structures on the heads of some animals that are used to sense the world around them

castes: groups (among ants) that have one main role, such as worker ants

colonies: groups of animals that live in close association with each other

crop: the part of an insect's digestive system where food can be stored

ecology: the study of the relationships between living creatures and their environments

entomologist: a scientist who studies insects

instinct: a natural tendency to act in a certain way without thinking about it

intelligence: the ability to understand and adapt to new situations

larvae: the wormlike immature stage of insects and other bugs

metamorphosis: the stages of development that an insect goes through to become an adult

naturalist: a person who investigates nature

prey: any animal grabbed by another animal for food

pupae: a stage in the development of insects between the larval stage and adulthood

species: a group of animals with common traits, especially the means of creating young

zoology: the study of animals

CHILEAN ROSEY TARANTULA

Bibliography

Cadwallader, Thomas C. and Christopher Joyce. "America's First Black Comparative Psychologist and Animal Behaviorist." Unpublished paper, Indiana State University, 1975.

Du Bois, W.E.B. "Men of the Month—C.H. Turner." *The Crisis.* January 1912.

———. "Postscript." *The Crisis.* June 1929.

Foerste, August F. "The Earlier History of the Bulletin of Scientific Laboratories of Denison University." *The Journal of the Scientific Labs of Denison University* 29 (1934).

Gerber, David A. *Black Ohio and the Color Line: 1860-1915.* Urbana: University of Illinois Press, 1976.

* Hayden, Robert. *Seven Black American Scientists.* New York: Addison Wesley, 1970.

Herrick, Charles Judson. "Clarence Luther Herrick." *Transactions of the American Philosophical Society* 45, part 1 (1955): 85.

Manning, Kenneth R. *Black Apollo of Science: The Life of Ernest Everett Just.* New York: Oxford University Press, 1983.

* McKissack, Patricia and Fredrick McKissack. *African American Scientists.* Brookfield, Connecticut: Millbrook Press, 1994.

Rau, Phil. "Dr. Charles Henry Turner." *Entomological News* 34, no. 10 (December 1923): 289-292.

Turner, Charles Henry. "Psychological Notes upon the Gallery Spider." *The Journal of Comparative Neurology* 2 (September 1892): 95-110.

———. "The Homing of Ants: An Experimental Study of Ant Behavior." *The Journal of Comparative Neurology and Psychology* 17, no. 5 (September 1907): 367-434.

———. "Experiments on Color Vision of the Honey Bee." *Biological Bulletin* 19, no. 5 (October 1910): 257-279.

———. "Experiments on Pattern-Vision of the Honey Bee." *Biological Bulletin* 21, no. 5 (October 1911): 249-264.

———. "Behavior of the Common Roach (Periplaneta orientalis l.) on an Open Maze." *Biological Bulletin* 25 (1913): 348-365.

———. "Notes of the Behavior of the Ant-lion with Emphasis on the Feeding and Letisimulation." *Biological Bulletin* 29, no. 5 (November 1915): 277-307.

Turner, Jean. Telephone conversations with the author, 1994.

* Asterisk indicates a book for younger readers.
All quotations in this book are taken from the above sources.

Index

Photographs and additional illustrations are reproduced through the courtesy of: Association for the Study of African American Life and History, Inc., front cover and p. 4; Cincinnati Historical Society, pp. 7, 10; Library of Congress, p. 19 (both); Academy of Science of St. Louis and the St. Louis Science Center, pp. 23, 26, 44 (top); Jean Turner, p. 36 (all); Biological Bulletin, pp. 38, 40; and St. Louis Schools Archives, p. 44 (bottom).

Ross, Michael Elsohn.
Bug watching.